JUMBO

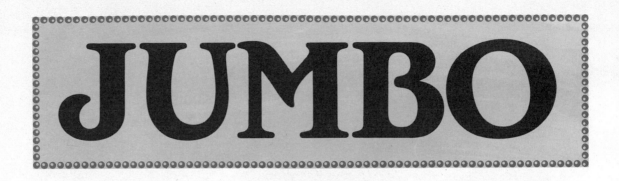

JUMBO

by Rhoda Blumberg
illustrated by Jonathan Hunt

BRADBURY PRESS   NEW YORK

Maxwell Macmillan Canada   Toronto
Maxwell Macmillan International
New York   Oxford   Singapore   Sydney

A NOTE ABOUT THE ART

The illustrations for *Jumbo* were done on 140 lb. hot press watercolor paper, using transparent
watercolors. The illustrations were color-separated by scanner and reproduced in four colors, using
red, blue, yellow, and black inks.

Bradbury Press
Macmillan Publishing Company
866 Third Avenue
New York, NY 10022

Maxwell Macmillan Canada, Inc.
1200 Eglinton Avenue East
Suite 200
Don Mills, Ontario M3C 3N1

Macmillan Publishing Company is part of the Maxwell Communication Group of Companies.

First edition
Printed and bound in the United States of America
10 9 8 7 6 5 4 3 2 1
The text of this book is set in 16 pt Goudy Oldstyle.
Typography by Julie Y. Quan

LIBRARY OF CONGRESS CATALOGING-IN-PUBLICATION DATA
Blumberg, Rhoda.
        Jumbo / by Rhoda Blumberg. — 1st ed.
                p.   cm.
        Summary: With his friend and trainer Matthew Scott, Jumbo, the
giant African elephant, leaves his home at the London Zoo and
becomes part of the P. T. Barnum circus.
        ISBN 0-02-711683-2
        1. Jumbo (Elephant)—Juvenile literature.   2. Circus—Juvenile
literature.   [1. Jumbo (Elephant)   2. Elephants.]   I. Title.
GV1831.E4B58   1992
791.3′2—dc20   91-34789

For my sister, Cynthia, and my brother, Eddie
       —R.B.

For Annelies and David Behnke,
who, as parents, know
the true meaning of the word "circus"
       —J.H.

When he was only a baby, a tiny elephant was captured in the African jungle. An animal dealer bought him, then sold him to France's most elegant zoo, the *Jardin des Plantes* in Paris. The little fellow was neglected by keepers who didn't bother to feed and clean him properly. He became scrawny, sickly, and sad-looking. Bigger, more beautiful elephants attracted all the crowds.

Matthew Scott had been cleaning animal cages and feeding birds and beasts at the Royal Zoological Gardens in London, England, for twenty years. Scott was a poor, lonely, middle-aged bachelor who felt unimportant and unloved.

Then the wheel of fortune stopped at his number.

Because the London Zoo didn't own an African elephant, its directors arranged a swap. They sent a rhinoceros to the Paris Zoo. In return, the Paris Zoo sent their scrawny elephant—and threw in two anteaters to make it a fair exchange. Officials at England's Royal Zoological Gardens called their new attraction "Jumbo," because they thought the name sounded African.

Scott was chosen to be the keeper of this newly acquired four-year-old, four-foot-high elephant. Jumbo became the light of his life. Scott looked after him with all the care and affection of a mother and a father. He stroked his trunk, scrubbed him—even washed behind his ears—and fed him wholesome vegetarian foods. Matthew Scott was a changed man. He walked tall and felt proud. "I am happy in Jumbo's company," he declared.

Scott's devotion changed little Jumbo's personality. He had found someone to love, and he thrived. The elephant often used the "fingers" at the tip of his sensitive trunk to hold Scott's hand. Sometimes he gave his keeper an affectionate hug, by curling his long nose around Scott's waist.

Jumbo's love grew by leaps and bounds, and his body
expanded until it reached gigantic proportions.

He became the largest animal in captivity in the entire world. Eleven feet high, weighing seven tons, measuring eighteen feet around the waist, he was awesome.

Despite his huge size and powerful body, Jumbo was so
gentle and sweet-natured that a special saddle–platform
called a *howdah* was strapped to his back so that groups
of children could enjoy elephant rides.

Thousands of visitors fed him treats. They marveled at the delicate, dainty way he accepted candies and bits of bread from their hands. For seventeen years Jumbo's home address was Royal Zoological Gardens, Regent's Park, London, England. The British looked upon him as one of their national treasures.

However, when Jumbo reached the age of twenty-one, the zoo's directors became very concerned. They worried because large bull elephants can be dangerous to people. Jumbo had already shown that he could go wild when Scott wasn't close by. At night, when his keeper was away, the big-eared, long-nosed giant had tantrums. He damaged his cage by banging his body against its walls, and he broke his huge tusks when he jammed them into its metal bars. The prospect of Jumbo running amok in London was a nightmare. Keeping him seemed risky.

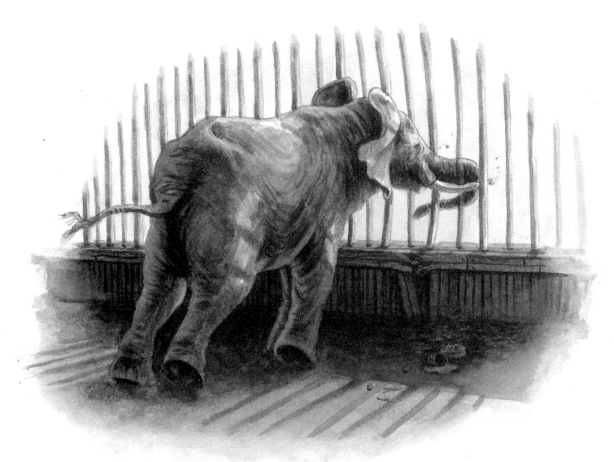

Fortunately, America's most famous showman, Phineas T. Barnum, was anxious to own Jumbo. This great circus impresario had featured Constantine, "the most tattooed person in the world," and Tom Thumb, "the smallest midget in the world." He now wanted Jumbo, "the largest animal in captivity."

How delighted he was to receive a cable from his London talent scout, informing him that the zoo's directors were willing to sell their jungle giant for two thousand pounds sterling (ten thousand dollars). Barnum immediately sent an agent across the Atlantic to deliver the money.

Newspaper reporters deplored the sale. The British were stunned. Queen Victoria was upset. The Prince of Wales expressed extreme displeasure. The sale of the nation's pet was criticized in the House of Commons. The United States ambassador stated at a banquet that "the only burning question between England and America is Jumbo."

Dinner parties were disturbed.
Children and their parents sent hundreds of letters begging the government to buy back the elephant.

Some of the zoo directors felt so awful that they brought the matter to court, hoping they could keep Jumbo. But Mr. Justice Chitty was sorry to say that he had no legal power to stop the sale. Jumbo's fate was sealed. England mourned.

Barnum was ecstatic. His expert animal trainer, "Elephant Bill" Newman, sailed to England to bring back the elephant. Swaggering about, feeling very important, Newman was positive he could control and command any animal, anywhere.

To make the elephant more manageable, heavy chains were wrapped around his head and front legs. Elephant Bill prodded him with a steel hook. Then he tried to lure him with sugar buns, Jumbo's favorite food. It was useless. Jumbo was stubborn. He refused to budge.

Elephant Bill was desperate. He was also embarrassed, because he had to ask Scott—a lowly zoo attendant—for help.

As soon as Scott took charge, Jumbo willingly walked to the zoo's entrance gate.

But then he threw himself down on the pavement.
He just lay there, trumpeting and groaning for one day
and one night.

Some newspaper reporters praised Jumbo as a great
patriot who didn't want to leave England. Others declared
that Jumbo couldn't bear to be separated from his sweet-
heart, Alice, the elephant who lived next door. What a lie!
Jumbo was not romantically interested in Alice.

Finally Scott was allowed to lead him back to his zoo-home.
Zoo officials realized that Scott was the only one who could control this bullheaded bull elephant. When they cabled Barnum about this, the smart Yankee showman hired Scott to continue on as Jumbo's keeper.

No one knew that Scott had signaled Jumbo to lie down by putting his fingers to his lips, and that he had ordered Jumbo to get up by whispering something in the animal's ear.

In the dark of night, a wagon-cage carrying Jumbo was pulled by ten horses to the London docks. Then it was ferried to the ocean liner SS *Assyrian Monarch*. Scott was perched on a platform in front of the cage, holding Jumbo's trunk, so that neither he nor the elephant felt fear. The two were separated briefly when Jumbo was hoisted high in the air by steam crane and lowered onto the ship's deck. The animal was terrified until he was reunited with Scott, who remained at his side during the entire ocean voyage.

After two weeks at sea, the ship docked at Battery Park, New York. Barnum's "Greatest Show on Earth" was playing uptown at Madison Square Garden.

Even though it was late at night, Barnum staged a spectacular parade to impress the public with Jumbo's gigantic size. First, hundreds of men yanked two ropes attached to Jumbo's wheeled cage, to start it rolling. Then, sixteen horses pulled the cage, and two elephants pushed it up Broadway. What a triumphant entrance to America's largest city! Crowds went wild cheering.

Jumbo became the star attraction of Barnum's circus. Clowns, tightrope walkers, and trapeze daredevils were entertaining, but thousands of people bought tickets just to see "the biggest beast on the face of the earth." There were other elephants in the circus. They wore pink ballet tutus, as they twirled on their hind legs, dancing to the music of the band. But these smaller-eared Asian-elephant ballerinas were not nearly as impressive as Jumbo, who didn't do any tricks. He just walked around the ring. All eyes were on this grand giant. He became famous, and his name, *Jumbo*, became a word meaning B-I-G.

Always on the lookout for a good publicity stunt, Barnum arranged for Scott to lead Jumbo across the Brooklyn Bridge—to prove that the one-year-old bridge would not break, even when a "mammoth" walked across it. Scott was nervous during the crossing, but he was proud of Jumbo, who calmly strolled over the East River from Manhattan to Brooklyn. His pet seemed to enjoy seeing boats beneath him. People jammed riverbanks and rooftops to gawk and gasp. They reacted as though the elephant and his keeper were tightrope walkers performing high in the air above a dangerous river.

The circus went on tour. Jumbo and Scott traveled in their own beautiful red-and-gold Palace Car. Scott rode in a compartment in front. A door separated it from the elephant's room. Jumbo often used his trunk to open the door. Scott didn't sleep well, but he didn't mind—except when Jumbo pulled off his blankets, lifted him out of bed, and set him on the floor.

Jumbo and Scott made over one hundred stops throughout North America. Whenever they could, they went swimming in rivers and streams. Scott would splash Jumbo. Jumbo would use his trunk to give Scott a shower.

What a wonderful sight to see! Here was an act that Barnum did not plan—a private performance that expressed pure pleasure.

A NOTE FROM THE AUTHOR

Phineas T. Barnum was, indeed, a legendary showman who specialized in legends. With the help of his publicity agents, he entertained people with preposterous exaggerations about his circus performers.

Even though Jumbo was truly a spectacular size, Barnum stretched the truth beyond belief. Posters depicted passengers in a horse-drawn carriage driving underneath Jumbo's stomach—with room to spare. Trade cards pictured people leaning out of a third-floor window to pet the elephant's trunk.

Newspaper reporters helped drum up "Jumbomania" by featuring outlandish tales about the animal. According to a spoof in the *New York Times*, Queen Victoria used to keep Jumbo outside her castle, "where she would often romp with him by the hour, making him fetch and carry like a dog and rolling with him in innocent delight upon the turf." At teatime the elephant used to "beg for lumps of sugar like a trained poodle." The Queen would also ride Jumbo in her "back yard." She would be seated on a howdah, while Prime Minister Benjamin Disraeli straddled the elephant's neck.

Manufacturers of soaps, sewing threads, cigars, and medicines used Jumbo's picture to advertise their products. Tradesmen sold "Jumbo-size" items, such as bonnets, bracelets, fans, and perfumes for ladies, and canes, hats, and neckties for men. They furnished free publicity for Barnum's star attraction, and caused the name Jumbo to become an adjective meaning oversized.

September 15, 1885, only three and a half years after arriving in America, Jumbo was accidentally struck and killed by a train. The circus had just performed at St. Thomas, Ontario. Jumbo and other elephants were being directed to their railroad cars when an unscheduled freight train rushed toward them. The other animals got out of the way in time. Scott shrieked, "Run, Jumbo, run." The elephant set off as fast as he could, but he ran on the tracks! When the engine slammed into Jumbo, the locomotive and several cars of the freight train were derailed and demolished.

Jumbo's death made front-page news throughout the world. Reporters embellished the story. Some said that Jumbo had deliberately rammed the train, because he viewed it as an enemy. Others adopted Barnum's creative fiction: that Jumbo had heroically sacrificed his own life when he pushed a tiny elephant named Tom Thumb from the oncoming locomotive.

In later years, Barnum donated Jumbo's skeleton to New York's American Museum of Natural History, and the mounted hide to Tufts University in Massachusetts. The bones remain at the museum. The hide was destroyed by fire in 1975.

After the accident Scott's spirit was broken. For many years he looked after small animals at the circus's winter quarters. During the 1900s he was discharged. He died in the Bridgeport, Connecticut, almshouse in 1914.

ABOUT THE RESEARCH

Reconstructing the *true* story of Jumbo was a challenge. Because Barnum was a master at "humbug," extracting fact from fiction proved to be a jumbo job. I tried, but please understand: I was under the spell of "the greatest showman on earth."

I referred to newspaper articles that appeared in the *New York Times* and the *Times* of London, from 1881 through 1885. I studied Barnum memorabilia at the Somers Historical Society of Somers, New York, and at the Lincoln Center Library of the Performing Arts and the New York Historical Society, both in New York City.

I read the following:

PRIMARY SOURCE BOOKS
Barnum, P. T. *Barnum's Own Story*. New York: Viking Press, 1927.

Scott, Matthew. *Autobiography of Matthew Scott, Jumbo's Keeper*. Bridgeport, CT: Trow's Printing and Bookbinding of New York, 1885.

SECONDARY SOURCE BOOKS
Harris, Neil. *Humbug, the Art of P. T. Barnum*. Chicago: University of Chicago Press, 1981.

Saxon, A. H., and P. T. Barnum. *The Legend and the Man*. New York: Columbia University Press, 1989.

Wallace, Irving. *The Fabulous Showman: The Life and Times of P. T. Barnum*. New York: Alfred A. Knopf, 1959.

MAGAZINE ARTICLES
Haley, James. "The Colossus of His Kind: Jumbo." *American Heritage*, December 1961.

Van Gelder, Richard. "A Big Pain: Whatever Was the Matter with Jumbo?" *Natural History*, March 1991.

ABOUT THE AUTHOR

RHODA BLUMBERG "shines in the imaginative use of extensive research to tell, compellingly and entertainingly, stories from history," says *School Library Journal*. A self-proclaimed "compulsive researcher" who calls her library card her "most valuable passport," the author's masterful presentations of landmark events in history include *Commodore Perry in the Land of the Shogun*, a 1986 Newbery Honor Book, which also won the *Boston Globe/Horn Book* Award and the Golden Kite Award; *The Incredible Journey of Lewis and Clark*, an ALA Notable Book and Golden Kite Award-winner; and, recently published, *The Remarkable Voyages of Captain Cook*, an ALA *Booklist* Editors Choice, a *School Library Journal* Best Book of the Year, and an ALA Notable Book.

The Great American Gold Rush, also an ALA Notable Book, won the John and Patricia Beatty Award, presented by the California Library Association. Accepting that award, Rhoda Blumberg said, "Stories are enchanting, and for me, true stories—from history—are the most enchanting. History is a record of human behavior—the most fascinating subject of all."

The author and her husband, Gerald, live in New York State's Westchester County.

ABOUT THE ARTIST

JONATHAN HUNT's first book, *Illuminations*, which he both wrote and illustrated, shows his love for history and research. It was called "elegant support for units on the Middle Ages" by *Booklist*, and *Perspectives* said, "*Illuminations* takes its place in the Alphabet Hall of Fame."

For *The Mapmaker's Daughter*, by M. C. Helldorfer, Mr. Hunt undertook an imaginative journey of his own, researching the art, costumes, architecture, and plant life of several Eastern lands, including ancient Persia, Saudi Arabia, and India.

Jonathan Hunt began his research for *Jumbo* by looking at "the many colorful posters and lithographic advertisements showing Jumbo and other nineteenth-century circus performers." He was also influenced by "the naturalistic and often emotional styles of William Holman Hunt, John W. Waterhouse, and Edwin Austin Abbey, artists who were working during Jumbo's career."

A graduate of Paier College of Art, the artist and his wife, Lisa, live in Claremont, New Hampshire.